An Itinerary Companion to Must-See Sights, Explore Hidden Gems in Penang

Penang
Travel Guide 2023

Curtis Kerr

All Rights Reserved!

No part of this book may be reproduced, stored in a retrieval system, or transmitted in any form or by any means, electronic, mechanical, photocopying, recording, or otherwise, without the prior written permission of the copyright owner.

Copyright 2023, Curtis Kerr.

Table of Contents

INTRODUCTION
  Welcome to Penang
  History of Penang
  About this Guide

II. PLANNING YOUR TRIP
  Weather and Best Time to Visit Penang
  Getting to Penang
  Visa Requirements
  Currency and Money Tips
  Penang Transportation Options
  Options for Accommodation

III. EXPLORING GEORGE TOWN
  Georgetown Heritage Area
  Street Art Trail
  Penang Peranakan Mansion
  Khoo Kongsi Clan House
  Kapitan Keling Mosque
  Cheong Fatt Tze Mansion (Blue Mansion)

Explore Penang 3

III. DISCOVERING PENANG HISTORICAL CULTURE
- Kek Lok Si Temple
- Snake Temple
- Dhammikarama Burmese Temple
- St. George's Church
- Penang State Museum and Art Gallery

V. UNCOVERING PENANG'S NATURAL BEAUTY
- Penang Hill
- Penang National Park
- Batu Ferringhi Beach
- Tropical Spices Park
- Escape Adventureplay Theme Park

VI. TASTING PENANG'S CULINARY DELIGHTS

VII. DAY TRIPS FROM PENANG

VIII. PRACTICAL INFORMATION AND TIPS
- Useful Phrases
- Helpful Contacts and Websites
- Security And Safety Tips

Medical and Health Facilities
Customs and Etiquettes

IX. TRAVELING IN PENANG WITH KIDS

X. IDEAL PENANG ITINERARIES

XI. CONCLUSION
Penang's Dos and Don'ts
Penang FAQs

INTRODUCTION

Welcome to Penang

The enchanting island of Penang, sometimes known as the "Pearl of the Orient," is situated off the northwest coast of Peninsular Malaysia. Penang has gained popularity as a vacation destination due to its fascinating history, lively culture, breathtaking scenery, and delectable food.

Georgetown, the capital of the island, is recognized as a UNESCO World Heritage Site and is famed for its exquisite colonial architecture, charming shophouses, and eye-catching street art. Discovering Georgetown's winding alleyways is like traveling back in time; they are lined with busy markets, temples, mosques, and churches that represent the island's rich cultural past.

With influences from Malay, Chinese, Indian, and European traditions, Penang is a cultural melting pot. Its culinary culture reflects this combination, making Penang a haven for foodies. The island provides a variety of tastes and meals that are guaranteed to entice your taste buds, from flavorful street food booths to upmarket eateries.

Penang has stunning natural beauty that is just waiting to be discovered beyond the busy streets of Georgetown. To find beautiful beaches, rich rainforests, and a variety of species, visit the Penang National Park or climb Penang Hill for stunning views of the metropolis and shoreline.

Penang is a gateway to other adjacent locations in addition to its cultural and natural features. You may take day excursions to the picturesque Cameron Highlands, Ipoh, Taiping, or Langkawi

Island, which is renowned for its beautiful beaches.

Penang provides a unique and remarkable experience, whether you're looking for historical sites, gastronomic excursions, natural marvels, or a combination of all three. Penang is a place that shouldn't be missed because of its friendly people, fascinating history, and alluring attractions.

History of Penang

Penang's long-standing history is entwined with the rise and fall of several empires, trading routes, and colonial forces. The major historical occurrences that have influenced the island's history are summarized as follows:

Early Settlements: Indigenous Malay tribes lived on the island of Penang before the advent of the Europeans. As a result of its advantageous position beside the maritime trade routes of the Straits of Malacca, it functioned as a significant commercial center for Malay, Chinese, and Indian traders.

British Settlement: In 1786, British East India Company Captain Francis Light established a trade base on Penang Island. With this, British dominance in the area officially began. In a deal with the Sultan of Kedah, Light acquired the island in return for defense against Siamese and Burmese assaults.

Colonial Period: Penang prospered as a significant trade port during British control. A diversified and cosmopolitan culture was created as a consequence of immigration brought about by the British government from China, India, and numerous other Southeast Asian countries. Penang was a significant commerce hub for goods including opium, tea, tin, and spices due to its advantageous position and natural harbor.

Japanese Occupation: From 1941 until 1945, Japan occupied Penang and the rest of Malaya during World War II. For the inhabitants of the island, the Japanese occupation was a difficult time that was characterized by privation, forced labor, and brutality.

Post-Independence: Following the conclusion of World War II, Penang joined the Federation of Malaya, which became free of British colonial authority in 1957. Penang remained a key business center, and Malaysia's economic development benefited greatly from its industrialisation.

The city of Georgetown, which serves as Penang's capital, was named a UNESCO World Heritage Site in 2008. Its well-preserved colonial architecture, distinctive cultural legacy, and historical importance as a commercial harbor all contributed to its designation.

Penang is known today as a thriving, international city where the past and present coexist together. The island's rich cultural variety continues to draw visitors from all over the globe to its architecture, religious monuments, festivals, and culinary customs.

The endurance, diversity, and ongoing heritage of Penang's colonial and commercial past are shown through its history. It serves as evidence of the island's distinctive character and its status as a compelling vacation spot for travelers looking for both historical and modern experiences.

About this Guide

The thorough reference "Penang Travel Guide 2023: An Itinerary Companion to Must-See Sights, Explore Hidden Gems in Penang' in Penang" was created to help tourists plan their trip to Penang, Malaysia. This travel manual strives to provide you with current and useful information so you can get the most out of your visit to this alluring island.

The guide includes an introduction of Penang, its history, culture, and food, among other subjects. It offers helpful advice on how to organize your trip, including the best time to visit, travel alternatives, visa needs, and lodging possibilities.

The book showcases Penang's must-see sights and little-known jewels, such as its historical sites, cultural hubs, scenic locales, and gastronomic hotspots.

Along with well-known locations like Georgetown, Penang Hill, and Batu Ferringhi Beach, it also has lesser-known gems that provide uncommon experiences.

The guide also recommends day excursions from Penang to adjacent locations so you may extend your schedule and explore the region. Additionally, you'll discover useful details on how to buy, regional traditions and etiquette, language and communication hints, safety and health issues, and more.

This guide attempts to cater to your interests and assist you in making long-lasting memories during your trip to Penang, whether you're a history buff, culinary lover, nature adventurer, or just seeking an engaging cultural experience. While we make every effort to provide accurate and trustworthy information, please be aware that certain information, such as operation hours, ticket rates, and availability, may be subject to change.

II. PLANNING YOUR TRIP

Weather and Best Time to Visit Penang

The whole year, Penang has a tropical climate with frequent rains, high humidity, and warm temperatures. Planning your trip and making the most of your time on the island might be made easier by being aware of the weather trends. An overview of Penang's climate and the ideal time to visit is provided below:

- Due to the comparatively milder and drier weather, Penang has its busiest travel season from December to February. There is little rain and temperatures vary from 23°C (73°F) to 32°C (90°F). It's a great season for outdoor activities, seeing sights, and taking advantage of the stunning beaches. However, be aware that hotels and tourist attractions can be busier during this time.

- **Hot Season (March to May):** From 24°C (75°F) to 33°C (91°F), on average, are the hotter months of March to May. High humidity levels make it possible for sporadic showers or thunderstorms. Despite the heat, this time of year continues to draw travelers who want to experience Penang's sights, cuisine, and cultural activities. It's wise to drink plenty of water, look for shade, and schedule inside activities for when it's hot outside.

- **The inter-monsoon season**, which lasts from June to August, is characterized by both bright days and brief downpours. Between 24°C (75°F) to 32°C (90°F), the temperature ranges, while the humidity is consistently high. Even though it happens more often at this time, the rain normally falls in brief spurts and doesn't usually interfere with travel arrangements. If you don't mind the occasional rains and wish to avoid greater crowds, now is a fantastic time to go to Penang.

- **Rainy Season (September to November):** Penang has its rainy season during the southwest monsoon, which brings more rain and higher humidity. Even though the rain may be quite heavy, it often comes in short spurts or in the nights, giving you plenty of opportunity to explore throughout the day. With fewer people around and maybe cheaper accommodation prices, this time of year is known as the low tourist season.

- **The dry season,** which lasts from December to February, is often the greatest time to visit Penang since the weather is good and you can enjoy outdoor activities without worrying about getting wet. Penang is a year-round destination because of its attractions and energetic environment, so you may tailor your trip to your tastes and level of tolerance for heat or precipitation.

Remember that weather patterns may change and that unforeseen weather occurrences might occur. Prior to your journey, it is advised to check the local weather forecast and carry the proper clothes and accessories, such as sunscreen and an umbrella.

Getting to Penang

Penang's well-connected transportation system makes getting there rather easy. The main methods for getting to Penang are as follows:

By Air: The major entry point to the island is Penang International Airport (PEN), which is serviced by both local and foreign airlines. Several regional as well as large cities in Malaysia are served by several airlines that provide direct flights to Penang. You may quickly get from the airport to your lodging using a taxi, ride-hailing services, or hotel transfers.

By car: You may go to Penang by car if you are already in Malaysia or one of its surrounding nations. The North-South Expressway links Penang to a number of Malaysian cities. To get to the island, you may either drive your own car or rent a car. Regular bus and coach services are also provided from other locations around the nation, including Kuala Lumpur, Singapore, and other significant cities, to Penang.

By Train: There isn't a direct train that goes to Penang, but you may take one to Butterworth, which is on the mainland and is situated next to Penang Island. A boat or the Penang Bridge may be used to go to

Georgetown from Butterworth, a significant transportation center. Train travel to Butterworth from Kuala Lumpur and other Malaysian cities is convenient and beautiful.

Ferry: From Butterworth, you may board a ferry to Penang Island if you're coming from the mainland. The boat service runs often, and the trip takes 15 to 20 minutes. A well-liked and reasonably priced method of transportation, ferries provide stunning views of the coastline and Georgetown's cityscape.

By Cruise: Penang is a well-liked stop for cruise ships traveling through the area. Many cruise companies include Penang into their itineraries, enabling passengers to spend a day or more exploring the island.

Taxis, ride-hailing services, buses, and rental vehicles are just a few of the alternatives for getting about the island after you get to Penang. It is simple to travel about in Georgetown and other large cities because of their well-established public transit systems.

Checking the most recent travel alternatives and timetables is advised, particularly during busy times of year or when there are specific travel warnings or advisories in effect.

Visa Requirements

Depending on your country of citizenship and the planned duration of your stay, different visas are needed to enter Penang, Malaysia. The necessary visas for the most frequent visitors are summarized below:

- **Visa Waivers:** For a limited time, several nations' citizens are permitted to travel without a visa. Tourists are permitted to visit Malaysia, including Penang, without a visa during certain exemptions, which normally last between 14 and 90 days. The United States, Canada, the United Kingdom, Australia, New Zealand, most of the European Union countries, and many more are among the nations that do not need visas for tourists. Before departing, you should confirm the length of the visa exemption and any additional requirements with the Malaysian diplomatic post or consulate in your country.

- **Visa on Arrival:** Individuals from a select group of nations may enter Malaysia without a visa. The availability of this facility, which permits stays of up to 30 days, is often found at important entrance points, like Penang International Airport. It's crucial to remember that not all nations qualify for a visa on arrival, so it's best to check the prerequisites ahead of time.

You must apply for a visa in advance of coming to Malaysia if your nation is not qualified for visa on arrival or visa exemption. You may apply for a single-entry tourist visa at the Malaysian embassy or consulate that is most conveniently located in your home country.

A valid passport, a filled-out application form, passport-sized pictures, documentation of your travel and lodging plans, and enough money to cover your stay in Malaysia are normally needed to apply for a visa.

It's essential to confirm the most recent laws and procedures for obtaining a visa since they are subject to change and your nationality may have different requirements. For the most recent details and advice on visa requirements for your particular situation, see the official website of the Malaysian Immigration Department or get in touch with the closest Malaysian diplomatic mission or consulate.

To prevent any issues, it's also a good idea to make sure your passport is valid for at least six months beyond the duration of your anticipated stay in Malaysia.

Currency and Money Tips

The Malaysian Ringgit (MYR) is the country of Malaysia's official currency. Here are some crucial details about money and currencies in Penang:

- **Currency Exchange:** Banks, licensed money changers, and currency exchange booths are all places where you may exchange foreign currency for Malaysian Ringgit. These amenities are easily accessible at well-known tourist destinations, airports, and retail centers. To get the most for your money, it is advised to compare exchange rates and costs. Additionally, it's a good idea to have some Malaysian Ringgit on hand for smaller businesses or locations that may not take cards.

- Automated teller machines (ATMs) are extensively dispersed throughout Penang, and the majority of them accept debit and credit cards from outside. Using your card, you may withdraw Malaysian Ringgit straight from ATMs. To make sure your card will operate abroad and to find out whether there are any fees or charges for foreign withdrawals, it is advised to contact your bank before leaving.

- **Credit Cards:** The majority of hotels, restaurants, shopping centers, and other significant enterprises in Penang accept major credit cards including Visa, MasterCard, and American

Express. Local marketplaces and smaller businesses can prefer cash payments. To prevent any possible problems with card use, it is important to let your credit card company know about your vacation intentions.

- **Tipping:** Although not required in Malaysia, good service merits a tip. The bill may contain a service fee at restaurants and motels. If not, it is common to tip 10% or so of the whole amount. Although it is not required, tips may also be given to tour guides, taxi drivers, and porters.

- **Budgeting:** Depending on your tastes and travel style, the cost of travel in Penang might vary. Budget-friendly to upscale alternatives are available for lodging, restaurants, and sightseeing. While posh restaurants and foreign cuisines might be somewhat more costly, street food stands and regional eateries provide more reasonable eating options. You may better organize your costs by creating a daily budget based on your tastes and doing pricing research beforehand.

- **Safety and Security:** To reduce the danger of theft or fraud, it is important to adopt the required measures while handling cash or using ATMs. Use ATMs only in well-lit, safe locations, and always cover your PIN while entering it. Always count your money before leaving the counter while exchanging it with strangers or illegitimate businesses.

For ease and security during your trip to Penang, it is advised that you check the most recent currency rates, keep track of your spending, and make sure you have a variety of payment alternatives (cash and cards).

Penang Transportation Options

Penang has a variety of means of transportation to make it easy for you to go about the island. The primary forms of transportation in Penang are as follows:

- **Public Buses:** Penang has a sizable public bus network that serves the city's main cities, tourist destinations, and neighborhoods. The primary bus company in Penang is Rapid Penang, and its buses are color-coded for various routes. Bus prices are reasonably priced, and you may pay with cash as you board the vehicle. It is simple to organize your trips thanks to the availability of timetables and route maps online and at bus stations.

- **Taxis** are accessible all across Penang, and you can either hail one or rent one from a marked taxi station. It's a good idea to insist on utilizing the taxi meter or haggle the price before leaving. Since Penang taxis don't often use meters, it's crucial to agree on a fee in advance. There are also ride-hailing services like Grab that provide a practical and often less expensive alternative to standard taxis.

- **Trishaws**: In Penang, notably in Georgetown, trishaws—also referred to as "beca" or tricycles—are a common method of transportation. Trishaws are often utilized for quick trips and tourism excursions. Prepare for a nostalgic and unhurried trip by haggling the fee in advance.

- **Rental Car:** You may explore Penang at your own leisure if you rent a vehicle. You may locate automobile rental agencies on the island at the airport, main cities, and popular tourist destinations. Make sure your driver's license is up to date and be aware that driving in Penang is done on the left-hand side of the road. It's essential to verify parking facilities before visiting well-known sites since parking places may be few in certain locations.

- **Cycling** is growing more and more popular in Penang, where there are designated lanes and rental options in certain places. Particularly in Georgetown and in the picturesque coastal regions, renting a bicycle may be an enjoyable and environmentally beneficial way to explore the island.

- **Ferries**: From Butterworth to Georgetown, you may use a ferry to transit between the mainland and Penang Island. The boat service runs often and provides a relaxing trip with lovely coastal views. At the ferry ports, you may buy ferry tickets.

Take into account the travel times, travel distances, and traffic situations while organizing your transportation in Penang. Checking timetables, planning your routes beforehand, and allowing additional time are also recommended, especially during busy times or tourist seasons.

Options for Accommodation

Penang has a variety of lodging choices to fit different travel interests, budgets, and styles. The following are some common options for lodging in Penang:

Penang has a wide variety of hotels and resorts that can accommodate a range of spending plans and tastes. In well-known locations like Georgetown, Batu Ferringhi, and Tanjung Bungah, you may choose from a broad selection of lodging choices, from five-star luxury hotels to affordable alternatives. These hotels often provide cozy accommodations, convenience to neighboring activities, and amenities like restaurants and swimming pools.

Penang is renowned for its quaint boutique hotels that provide distinctive experiences and honor the island's illustrious past. These upscale boutique hotels often include chic furnishings, attentive service, and a homey atmosphere. In Georgetown, there are several boutique hotels housed in historic structures, making for an engaging and genuine stay.

Guesthouses & Homestays: Guesthouses and homestays are great choices for a more personal and authentic experience. These lodgings, which are often managed by locals, provide cozy rooms or flats with a homey touch. A guesthouse or homestay may provide a chance to learn about the customs and culture of the area as well as to engage with welcoming hosts.

Hostels: There are several hostels in Penang for backpackers and visitors on a tight budget. Hostels provide dormitory-style lodging with shared amenities including common rooms and kitchens. They are an inexpensive choice for those who are traveling alone or who want to socialize with other tourists.

Service Apartments: If you'd want additional room and self-catering amenities, this is an easy option. These flats often include a living room, a kitchenette or complete kitchen, and separate bedrooms. They are appropriate for families or tourists who seek a setting that feels like home while they are away.

When choosing a place to stay in Penang, take into account elements like location, accessibility to amenities and public transportation, facilities and amenities provided, and internet testimonials from prior visitors. To ensure the greatest pricing and availability, it is advised to make reservations in advance, particularly during the busiest travel times.

Additionally, do some research on the area of Penang in which you want to stay as various areas offer different experiences. Batu Ferringhi is well-known for its beaches and resort-style lodgings, but Georgetown is well-known for its history and cultural attractions. Popular neighborhoods with a variety of lodging options and convenient access to services and activities include Tanjung Bungah and Gurney Drive.

Overall, Penang has a wide variety of lodging choices to suit all tastes and price ranges, assuring a relaxing and pleasurable stay on the island.

III. EXPLORING GEORGE TOWN

Georgetown Heritage Area

A UNESCO World Heritage Site, Georgetown Heritage Area in Penang is recognized for its extensive history, varied influences, and beautifully maintained buildings. To assist you in discovering this intriguing region, the following is thorough descriptive travel information:

Background and History:
The British founded Penang's capital, Georgetown, in 1786, and it swiftly developed into a prosperous trade harbor. It has drawn immigrants from China, India, the Middle East, and Europe throughout the years, creating a varied cultural tapestry that is reflected in the city's architecture, customs, and food scene. Due to its exceptional global importance, Georgetown was designated a UNESCO World Heritage Site in **2008.**

Heritage Route Maps:
The greatest way to experience Georgetown's historic aura is by walking about the city. A map of the Georgetown Heritage Area is available at tourist information offices or at your place of lodging. Important locations, pedestrian routes, and tourist attractions are often highlighted on the map. Explore the area's hidden jewels, historic structures, and vivid street art by following the authorized history routes.

Colonial building design
Colonial-era structures inspired by British, Chinese, Indian, and Islamic architectural styles may be seen in impressive numbers in Georgetown. A stroll along Armenian Street, Beach Street, or Lebuh Pantai will let you take in the exquisite shophouses, governmental structures, and clan homes with their unique façade, vibrant tiles, and elaborate embellishments. Fort Cornwallis,

the Town Hall, and the Penang State Museum are notable sites.

The Clan Jetties
The clan jetties are distinctive waterfront towns that provide visitors a look at the early Chinese immigration populations. Several Chinese tribes call these wooden jetties home, each with an own personality. Discover the traditional homes, regional practices, and bustling activity at Chew Jetty, Lee Jetty, and other jetties. Along the jetties, you could also come across gift stores, little cafés, and art galleries.

Mosques and Temples:
Temples and mosques may be found all across Georgetown, illustrating the wide range of religions practiced there. With its towering pagoda, beautiful sculptures, and expansive views of the city, the Kek Lok Si Temple, the biggest Buddhist temple in Southeast Asia, is a must-see destination.

Sri Mahamariamman Temple, Kapitan Keling Mosque, and St. George's Church are a few more revered places of worship.

Murals and Street Art:
Street art is a thriving industry in Georgetown. Be sure to see the well-known paintings by the Lithuanian artist Ernest Zacharevic, which mix in well with the city's historic surroundings. Explore Armenian Street and the nearby alleyways at your leisure to find these fascinating pieces of art that represent the history and culture of the area. Don't forget to take some priceless pictures!

Gastronomic Delights
Georgetown offers a beautiful combination of cuisines from several cultures, making it a food lover's heaven. Try Char Kuey Teow, Assam Laksa, and Hokkien Mee, some of Penang's most well-known street foods, in hawker areas like Gurney Drive or New Lane. Discover quaint cafés, eateries, and

regional specialties on Armenian Street, Chulia Street, and Kimberley Street to tempt your palate.

Galleries and Museums:
Visit the museums and galleries to fully immerse yourself in Penang's history and culture. A sizable collection of antiquities and works of art are kept at the Penang State Museum and Art Gallery, which offers insights into the state's history. The Upside Down Museum offers a unique interactive experience, while the Pinang Peranakan Mansion gives a look into the lavish lifestyle of the Straits Chinese population.

Cultural Festivals and Events:
Festivals and cultural events bring Georgetown to life. Through numerous concerts, displays, and seminars, the annual George Town Festival honors arts, culture, and tradition. Other noteworthy occasions that highlight the cultural variety and religious passion of the surrounding towns

include the Thaipusam celebration at the Waterfall Temple and the Hungry Ghost celebration.

Night Entertainment:
As dusk falls, Georgetown becomes a thriving center for entertainment and nightlife. To locate hip clubs, places to hear live music, and hopping night markets, go to Upper Penang Road or Love Lane. After a day of exploring, relax in the bustling environment and socialize with locals and other tourists.

As Georgetown's history region requires a lot of walking and outdoor exploring, make sure to pack appropriate shoes, water, sunscreen, and a hat. Enjoy the tastes of this alluring World Heritage Site, take in the history, and embrace the ethnic charm.

Street Art Trail

Discovering and appreciating the thriving street art culture in the city is made possible by participating in the Street Art Trail in Georgetown, Penang. Here is a map to assist you in navigating the path and discovering the intriguing artworks:

Begin at Armenian Street
A fantastic place to begin your exploration of street art is Armenian Street. This famous boulevard is well-known for its quaint cafés, classic stores, and a wide variety of fascinating paintings. Start your adventure here and enjoy the lively environment.

Look for the murals by Ernest Zacharevic:
With his engaging and thought-provoking murals, famous Lithuanian artist Ernest Zacharevic has made his imprint on Georgetown. Find his well-known pieces, which include "Little Children on a Bicycle" and "Boy on a Bike," which have evolved

into defining images of Penang's street art culture. These murals often use actual things and encourage audience participation.

Discover the Neighboring Streets:
Explore the nearby streets and alleys as you continue your street art path. A few of the numerous roads with eye-catching paintings and art installations include Lebuh Armenian, Lebuh Ah Quee, and Lebuh Cannon. As you stroll through the vibrant and ethnically diverse districts, keep a lookout for hidden jewels.

Discover George Town's Marking Project:
The Marking George Town Project is a program that displays one-of-a-kind iron rod sculptures that are carefully positioned across the city. These sculptures capture the spirit of the community's culture and traditions by depicting images from Penang's everyday life. Be on the lookout for

these sculptures, which often include illuminating inscriptions that provide background and historical details.

Look Out for Steel Rod Parodies:
The steel rod caricatures that decorate Georgetown's walls with a sense of humor are another noteworthy aspect of the city's street art culture. These caricatures, which often cover street corners and building facades, portray regional scenery, people, and customs. As you wander the streets, keep an eye out for these wonderful inventions.

Visit Street Art Alleys:
Georgetown is home to some attractive street art lanes in addition to the murals and sculptures. Discover the little alleyways off Armenian Street, including Ah Quee Street and Muntri Street, where you may discover a ton of unusual installations, paintings, and smaller-scale pieces of art.

Get involved with 3D murals:
The street art movement in Georgetown is renowned for its captivating 3D murals that provide optical illusions and let you interact with the art. Look for these interactive murals, which are often situated close to well-known tourist destinations, and enjoy posing for pictures to capture the illusion.

Explore Undiscovered Gems:
Don't be afraid to go off the beaten road and explore the less-traveled alleys and alleyways while following the well-known street art trail. Off the beaten route is where you may make some of the most thrilling discoveries and even come across unexpected artwork like secret murals.

While touring the street art path, keep in mind to show respect for the artwork and the nearby homes. Enjoy the unique experience of learning about Georgetown's dynamic street art community as you take your time to admire the ingenuity and ability that went into these pieces of art.

Penang Peranakan Mansion

A fascinating museum that provides a look into the lavish way of life of the Peranakan population in Penang is the Penang Peranakan Mansion. What you should know about this historical gem is as follows:

Peranakan Culture: The Peranakan are descended from Chinese immigrants who settled in the area and married local Malays, giving them the names Straits Chinese or Baba-Nyonya. Their language, traditions, and way of life evolved into a distinctive synthesis of Chinese, Malay, and European elements. The Penang Peranakan Mansion exhibits the history and customs of this thriving neighborhood.

Construction and Design: The museum itself is a work of art in architecture and is housed in a gorgeously restored 19th-century palace. The mansion's beautiful carvings, elaborate tiling, and opulent furniture are a reflection of the luxury and grandeur of the Peranakan aristocracy. The building's architecture, which combines Chinese, Malay, and European elements, is lovely to look at.

Museum Displays: Visit the Penang Peranakan Mansion inside to see its extensive collection of antiques and relics. The painstaking decoration of the mansion's interior showcases the Peranakan way of life in the late 19th and early 20th century in each of its rooms. Admire the ornate furnishings, deft woodwork, exquisite porcelain, and decorative items that adorn the rooms, offering a look into the Peranakan aesthetic and culture.

Cultural Relevance: The museum focuses insight on the traditions, rituals, and social activities of the Peranakan population in addition to preserving its material culture. Through the displays and educational exhibits, discover more about the Peranakan wedding customs, ancestor worship, and the position of women in Peranakan culture. Learn more about the Peranakan culture and its contribution to Penang's ethnic fabric.

Presented Tours: Consider taking a tour of the Penang Peranakan Mansion with a guide to make the most of your trip. Expert guides provide insightful explanations of the architecture, importance, and history of the on show items. They may impart fascinating tales about the mansion's previous occupants and provide insight into Peranakan culture.

Merchandise Store and Café: After you've finished the museum, spend some time looking around the gift store, which sells a variety of things with Peranakan influences, such elaborately embroidered kebayas and beaded slippers. You may also stop by the museum's café to sip on something cool or try some Peranakan treats.

Accessible Location: Visitors may readily reach the Penang Peranakan Mansion since it is situated on Church Street in Georgetown. Many additional nearby sights, like Khoo Kongsi and the Street of Harmony, are accessible on foot. Taxis, Grab, or the free Rapid Penang CAT shuttle bus are just a few of the ways you may get to the home.

Visit the Penang Peranakan Mansion to fully experience the Peranakan community's rich cultural history. It is an engrossing historical tour that provides a look into the splendor and refinement of Peranakan life in Penang's colonial period.

Khoo Kongsi Clan House

In Georgetown, Penang, there is a historical Chinese clan temple and social hub called the Khoo Kongsi Clan House. Everything you need to know about this important cultural landmark is provided below:

Background and History: The Khoo clan, one of Penang's major Chinese clans, built the Khoo Kongsi Clan House in the 19th century. A Chinese clan organization or lineage group is referred to as a "kongsi" in this context. The Khoo Kongsi functioned as a gathering place for the members of the Khoo clan who immigrated from the Chinese province of Fujian to Penang.

Architectural Glamour: Famous for its excellent architectural style and detailed workmanship, the Khoo Kongsi Clan House.

Intricate sculptures of dragons, phoenixes, and other mythological animals decorate the Dragon Mountain Gate, the main entryway. The clan home reflects the combination of Chinese and Malay architectural forms with its elaborate ornamentation, fine woodwork, and vibrant ceramic tiles.

Clan History and Ancestral Cults: The Khoo clan members gathered in the Khoo Kongsi Clan House to revere their ancestors and take part in social and cultural events. A central courtyard, prayer rooms, ancestral rooms, and a performance space are all located inside the compound. These areas provide light on the clan's religious beliefs, customs, and history.

Collections and Exhibitions: A museum showcasing the history and traditions of the Khoo clan is also housed in the clan home. The museum showcases antiques, images, and records that reflect the clan's migration, growth in Penang, and cultural customs.

Visitors may learn more about the clan's history and their important place in the neighborhood.

Cultural Events and Performances: The Khoo Kongsi Clan House features cultural events and performances all through the year, including Chinese opera and displays of martial arts. Visitors have the opportunity to take part in these events and enjoy traditional Chinese performing arts while also being immersed in a dynamic cultural environment.

Restoration and Conservation: In order to maintain the Khoo Kongsi Clan House's historical and architectural value, extensive repair work has been done. With the repair effort, the clan home will continue to be a well-kept and accurate reflection of Penang's Chinese history.

Accessible Location: Visitors may readily reach the Khoo Kongsi Clan House because of its convenient location on Cannon Square in the center of Georgetown. Other sites like the Penang Street Art and the Cheong Fatt Tze Mansion are close by and can be reached on foot. Taxis, Grab, or the free Rapid Penang CAT shuttle bus are just a few of the ways you may get to the clan home.

Experiencing the Khoo clan's rich legacy and learning about Penang's Chinese population may both be done by visiting the Khoo Kongsi Clan House. For individuals who are interested in Penang's history and multicultural heritage, it is a must-visit location because of its gorgeous architecture, cultural exhibitions, and exciting events.

Kapitan Keling Mosque

In Georgetown, Penang, there is a famous Islamic religious building known as the Kapitan Keling Mosque, or Masjid Kapitan Keling. An summary of this historically important mosque is provided below:

Architecture and History: The Kapitan Keling Mosque, which was built in the early 19th century, is very important to Penang's Muslim population both historically and culturally. The title of the influential Indian Muslim community leader at the time is where the name "Kapitan Keling" of the mosque comes from. The mosque's architecture combines Islamic, Moorish, and Indian Muslim elements.

Special Design Features: The mosque's eye-catching design combines Penang Malay and conventional Islamic architectural elements. A large central dome, minarets, ornate arches, and ornamental tiles are some of its standout characteristics. The mosque's facade has a striking combination of green and white hues, while its interior features stunning stained glass windows, chandeliers, and calligraphy.

Facilities and Prayer Rooms: The Kapitan Keling Mosque has a variety of prayer rooms that can hold a sizable crowd of worshipers. Persian carpets and Islamic calligraphy decorate the main prayer hall. The mosque also has separate areas for men and women to worship and ablution (wudu) facilities.

Religious and Cultural Significance: The mosque is a key religious and cultural hub for Penang's Muslim population. It serves as a venue of worship, social interaction, and instruction. Visitors may see how devoted believers are at prayer times and get a feeling of spirituality in the peaceful setting of the mosque.

Preservation and Heritage: To retain its historical and architectural integrity, the Kapitan Keling Mosque has undergone a number of repair and preservation projects. These initiatives have made sure that the mosque will always be a significant representation of Penang's diverse cultural history and Islamic traditions.

Availability to Visitors: While the Kapitan Keling Mosque serves as a primary site of prayer, anybody wishing to tour and take in its stunning architecture and historical importance is welcome to do so. When visiting the mosque, visitors are urged to dress modestly and with respect, with ladies covering their heads. The history, Islamic customs, and community involvement of the mosque may all be covered in guided tours.

Location Accessible: The Kapitan Keling Mosque is conveniently situated on Georgetown's Jalan Kapitan Keling, making it accessible to tourists. Other sights like the Street of Harmony and the Cheong Fatt Tze Mansion are close by and may be reached on foot. The mosque is easily accessible by public transit, including taxis and buses.

The Kapitan Keling Mosque provides a unique chance to witness Penang's Islamic traditions and stunning architecture. It offers a place for spiritual reflection and cultural appreciation while showcasing the peaceful coexistence of many civilizations within Georgetown's eclectic fabric.

Cheong Fatt Tze Mansion (Blue Mansion)

Here is a description of the Cheong Fatt Tze Mansion, popularly referred to as the Blue Mansion, a famous old structure in Georgetown, Penang:

Background and History: The Cheong Fatt Tze Mansion was the home of Cheong

Fatt Tze, a well-known Chinese businessman and politician who was dubbed the "Rockefeller of the East" and had a huge impact on the growth of Penang and Southeast Asia.

Architectural Glamor: Its most recognizable feature is its indigo blue exterior, which gives it the nickname "Blue Mansion." The mansion spans three stories and features ornate carvings, intricate porcelain adornments, and a stunning courtyard. It is renowned for its distinctive architectural style, fusing traditional Chinese design with Western Art Deco influences.

Feng Shui Guidelines: Feng Shui concepts are incorporated into the architecture of the home, with features like a central courtyard to promote the flow of good energy, beautiful woodwork, and strategically placed windows to improve ventilation and natural light.

Restoration and Conservation: In order to preserve its historical and architectural significance, the Cheong Fatt Tze Mansion underwent extensive restoration work. The restoration work, which won the UNESCO Asia-Pacific Heritage Award, made sure that the mansion's original splendor was maintained. The mansion is now a living museum that displays the way of life and cultural heritage of the era.

Presented Tours: Visitors can learn about the mansion's history, architecture, and the life of Cheong Fatt Tze as well as about its distinctive features, the family's cultural practices, and Cheong Fatt Tze's legacy during guided tours of the mansion's fascinating interior, which are led by knowledgeable guides.

Exclusive Hotel: In addition to being a tourist destination, the Cheong Fatt Tze Mansion also serves as a boutique hotel, giving guests the chance to stay in one of the mansion's exquisitely restored rooms and take in the atmosphere of a bygone era.

Accessible Location: The Cheong Fatt Tze Mansion is located on Leith Street in Georgetown, making it convenient for visitors. It is close to other attractions like the Kapitan Keling Mosque and the Penang Street Art, and is easily accessible via public transportation, including taxis and buses.

Whether you choose to explore the mansion as a tourist or stay as a guest, it offers an unforgettable experience that highlights the rich history and charm of Penang. A trip to the Cheong Fatt Tze Mansion is a trip back in time, allowing you to appreciate the architectural brilliance and cultural heritage of the Blue Mansion.

III. DISCOVERING PENANG HISTORICAL CULTURE

Kek Lok Si Temple

In Air Itam, Penang, there is a wonderful Buddhist temple complex called Kek Lok Si Temple. Here is a description of this outstanding holy location:

Background and Importance: The "Temple of Supreme Bliss," also known as Kek Lok Si Temple, was built over many decades starting in 1890. It is one of the biggest Buddhist temples in Southeast Asia and is very important to the neighborhood's Chinese population. The temple functions as a place of prayer, a cultural hub, and a destination for pilgrims.

Construction marvel: The temple complex is a stunning mix of Chinese, Thai, and Burmese architectural styles that demonstrates a peaceful integration of several Buddhist traditions. The Pagoda of Rama VI, a striking seven-story edifice covered in ornate carvings, figures, and vibrant ceramic tiles, is the center of attention. The temple complex also has a large number of prayer rooms, gardens, and Buddha sculptures.

Statue of the Goddess of Mercy: The enormous bronze figure of Kuan Yin, popularly known as the Goddess of Mercy, is one of the attractions of the Kek Lok Si Temple. The monument is a key representation of compassion and mercy in Buddhism and measures an astounding 30 meters tall. To get a panoramic perspective of the region, visitors may ascend the steps that encircle the monument.

Celebrations & Festivals: Especially during Chinese New Year, celebrations bring life to the Kek Lok Si Temple. The "Lanterns and Lights" exhibit, which is a captivating display made up of thousands of lanterns and lights, is displayed around the temple complex. It is the perfect time to go and see the temple's lively environment thanks to the celebratory mood, colorful decorations, and cultural performances.

Turtle Freedom: The temple is particularly well-known for its turtle pond, where followers of the Buddhist religion release turtles as a gesture of kindness and to accrue karma. The process of liberating turtles is open to spectators, and they may even take part by releasing their turtles into the pond.

Food and Souvenir Stands: The temple complex is home to a large number of food and souvenir booths that sell a variety of local specialties, souvenirs, and things with Buddhist themes. These kiosks may be explored by visitors who want to buy crafts, souvenirs, and tasty foods.

Accessible Location: It takes around 30 minutes to travel from Georgetown to Air Itam, where the Kek Lok Si Temple is located on a hill. Public transit, a taxi, or a vehicle may take you there. A meandering route or an inclined lift from the foothills may be used to get to the shrine. Beautiful views of Penang Island and the surrounding hills are available from the location.

A tranquil and spiritual experience is offered by visiting the Kek Lok Si Temple, which also immerses tourists in Penang's rich Buddhist traditions and cultural history. For those seeking tranquility and a greater knowledge of Buddhism, the temple is a must-visit location due to its magnificent architecture, peaceful atmosphere, and panoramic vistas.

Snake Temple

Intriguing and distinctive, the Snake Temple, also called the Temple of the Azure Cloud, is a place of worship in Bayan Lepas, Penang. Here is a brief description of this fascinating temple:

Lore and History: The history of the Snake Temple is interesting and entwined with myth and mythology. It was constructed in the middle of the 19th century and honors Buddhist monk Chor Soo Kong, who was renowned for his healing abilities. Legend has it that poisonous snakes lived in the temple and took refuge with the monk. The snakes started to watch over the shrine as an act of appreciation.

Peaceful Scenery: The Snake Temple is surrounded by thick vegetation, creating a pleasant and peaceful atmosphere. Visitors are welcomed by a gorgeously planted courtyard with sculptures and incense burners as soon as they reach the temple premises. Traditional Chinese design features and beautiful wood carvings are shown in the temple's building.

Existence of Snakes: The Snake Temple is well-known for its resident snakes, as the name would imply. There are still a few poisonous pit vipers within the temple, even though the number of snakes has decreased over time. The majority of the time, these snakes are coiled around tree branches, altars, or in specified enclosures. These reptiles are available for visitors to gaze at from a safe distance.

Spiritual Exercises: The Snake Temple is still a bustling site of devotion that draws worshippers looking for blessings and recovery. The offering of prayers, burning of incense sticks, and making offerings to Chor Soo Kong are all things that visitors may see devotees doing. It's a chance to take part in the religious observances and ceremonies connected to this particular temple.

Snake Management: The Snake Temple gives visitors the chance to handle non-venomous snakes for a more daring experience. When visitors engage with the snakes, skilled handlers are on hand to direct them and guarantee their safety. The excitement and pleasure of this action enhance the temple visit.

Refreshment and Souvenir Stands: The temple complex also features gift stores where tourists may buy religious goods and mementos with snake themes. Additionally, there are food and beverage stands selling regional specialties, giving visitors the chance to sample Penang's delectable cuisine.

Accessible Location: About a 30-minute drive from Georgetown, near Bayan Lepas, is where you'll find the Snake Temple. There are plenty of parking spaces available, and it is conveniently accessible by vehicle or cab. The temple is also accessible by ride-hailing services and other forms of public transit.

A trip to the Snake Temple delivers a unique and remarkable experience since it combines mythology, religion, and the allure of snakes. The Snake Temple in Penang guarantees a unique and unforgettable experience, whether you're fascinated by the temple's history, eager to watch religious ceremonies, or hoping to come into contact with these serpentine animals.

Dhammikarama Burmese Temple

In Georgetown, Penang, the Dhammikarama Burmese Temple is a revered religious and cultural landmark that honors the longstanding Buddhist legacy of Burma. A summary of this fascinating temple is provided below:

Historical Relevance: Being the first Burmese Buddhist temple in Malaysia, the Dhammikarama Burmese Temple enjoys this distinction. It was constructed in 1803 and serves as the focal point, cultural center, and place of prayer for the Burmese population in Penang.

Construction Marvel: The temple's design is a lovely fusion of traditional Thai and Burmese elements. Visitors are greeted at the main entry gate, which is embellished with elaborate carvings and vibrant paintings, and led inside a tranquil and well-kept temple area. Beautiful Buddha sculptures, golden spires, and elaborate woodwork decorate the main prayer hall, showing the superb skill of Burmese craftspeople.

Stupas and Pagodas: The expansive Maha Pasadabhumi Gandhakuti, a seven-tiered pagoda that stores holy relics, is one of several pagodas and stupas scattered across the temple complex. These stupas and pagodas serve as centers for worshiping the Buddha, engaging in meditation, and offering prayers.

Calming Garden: The temple complex has a well-kept garden with lovely sculptures, vibrant flowers, and lush vegetation. Visitors may unwind, practice meditation, or just take in the calm and quiet of the surroundings in this serene garden.

Cultural Activities: In addition to being a site of prayer, the Dhammikarama Burmese Temple serves as a hub for cultural events. Buddhist lectures, meditation sessions, and cultural events showcasing Burmese customs, music, and dance are all open to visitors. These exercises provide a greater understanding of the cultural customs and Buddhism of Burma.

Devotion and Offerings: Visitors to the temple may see worshippers presenting sacrifices, igniting incense, and praying. The ambiance inside the temple is one of awe and devotion, giving visitors a chance to see the spiritual ceremonies and practices of Burmese Buddhism.

Accessible Location: Georgetown's Dhammikarama Burmese Temple is conveniently situated, making it accessible to tourists. Other sites include the Penang Street Art and the Wat Chayamangkalaram Thai Buddhist Temple are nearby. There are several public transit alternatives in the neighborhood, including taxis and buses.

A taste of the rich Burmese Buddhist culture and customs may be had by visiting the Dhammikarama Burmese Temple. The temple offers a pleasant and enlightening experience for spiritual searchers and those interested in discovering Penang's unique religious traditions, from its opulent architectural features to its tranquil garden and cultural events.

St. George's Church

St. George's Church is a noteworthy historical and architectural monument that is situated in Georgetown, Penang. Here is a description of this famous church:

Historical Relevance: The oldest Anglican church in Southeast Asia is St. George's Church. It was constructed in 1818 and has a significant historical value since it was essential to Penang's growth. The church has St. George's name, it is England's patron saint.

Architectonic Grace: The church's distinctive Palladian-style exterior complements its outstanding colonial architecture. The church has an air of elegance and timelessness because of its white-washed facade, which is enhanced by towering columns and a striking tower. Wooden benches, stained glass windows, and a regal chancel are all part of the interior's classic design.

Heritage Qualities: The long history of St. George's Church is reflected in a number of its historical elements. Numerous historic tombstones, some of which date back to the early 19th century, can be found in the graveyard and provide insight into Penang's colonial history. Another notable element that enhances the atmosphere is the church's 1887 pipe organ.

Services & Worship: St. George's Church is still a bustling site of worship for Penang's Anglican population. Visitors are welcome to these religious meetings, which are regularly conducted. The peaceful surroundings of the church provide a pleasant setting for meditation, prayer, and spiritual reflection.

Concerts and Cultural Events: The church also organizes a variety of cultural occasions, such as choir performances and music concerts. These performances highlight the skills of regional and international artists and provide guests with a chance to enjoy live music while appreciating the interior beauty and acoustics of the cathedral.

Accessible Location: The handy location of St. George's Church in the center of Georgetown makes it simple for guests to get there. Farquhar Street is where it is located, adjacent to other well-known sights including Fort Cornwallis and the Penang State Museum. There are several public transit alternatives in the neighborhood, including buses and taxis.

Historical Remarkable: St. George's Church is a significant piece of Penang's history as a historical site. History buffs and aficionados of architecture should go there because of its architectural importance and contributions to the religious and cultural milieu.

A chance to experience St. George's Church's spiritual atmosphere and get insight into Penang's colonial heritage is provided by a visit there. Visitors may immerse themselves in the rich history and cultural legacy connected with this renowned church whether they attend a service, explore the graveyard, or take in a cultural event.

Penang State Museum and Art Gallery

In Georgetown, Penang, there is a well-known cultural institution called the Penang State Museum and Art Gallery. An overview of this gallery and museum is provided below:

Historical Relevance: The Penang Museum, a historic structure built in 1821, serves as home to the Penang State Museum and Art Gallery. The museum is significant historically since it was the first structure created specifically to conserve and present Penang's rich cultural history.

Historical Exhibitions in Penang: The museum offers a variety of exhibits that explore Penang's history. The island's varied history, including its colonial period, commercial links, and cultural influences, is shown via galleries that include relics, images, papers, and interactive exhibits.

Artwork Collections: An excellent collection of paintings, sculptures, and installations of modern art can be seen at the Penang State Museum and Art Gallery. The art gallery exhibits the creations of regional and international artists, highlighting Penang's thriving artistic community.

Unique Exhibits: The museum also presents recurring special exhibits that focus on different facets of Penang's history, culture, and art, in addition to its permanent holdings. These exhibits often concentrate on certain topics, including holidays, customs, or important historical moments, giving visitors a fuller appreciation of Penang's cultural diversity.

Educational Initiatives: For visitors of all ages, the museum provides seminars, educational activities, and tours with guides. These initiatives seek to increase both inhabitants' and visitors' appreciation for the arts, history, and culture. They provide chances for participatory learning and practical application.

Heritage Structure: An architectural wonder in and of itself is the Penang State Museum and Art Gallery. The structure has colonial-style architecture characteristics including beautiful arches, imposing pillars, and elaborate ornamentation. The building's opulent exterior and roomy interior make it a suitable backdrop for housing the museum's artifacts.

Accessible Location: The museum is conveniently situated on Georgetown's Farquhar Street, making it accessible to tourists. Other noteworthy sites like St. George's Church and Fort Cornwallis are accessible by foot. There are public transit alternatives in the neighborhood, including buses and taxis.

The Penang State Museum and Art Gallery provide visitors with a thorough cultural experience, enabling them to learn more about the island's history, offers an invaluable platform to connect with Penang's past and present via historical relics and modern artworks, making it a must-visit location for history buffs, art lovers, and cultural explorers.

V. UNCOVERING PENANG'S NATURAL BEAUTY

Penang Hill

In Penang, Malaysia, Penang Hill, sometimes called Bukit Bendera, is a well-liked tourist attraction. Here is a description of this picturesque hill station:

Magnificent views: Penang Hill has stunning 360-degree views over Georgetown, Penang's mainland, and the surroundings. The beautiful skyline, rich vegetation, and glittering seas of the Strait of Malacca are all breathtaking vistas that may be enjoyed by tourists. The hill's elevation offers a welcome respite from the busy metropolis below.

Railroad Funicular: The funicular train, a century-old railway system that takes tourists from the base to the peak, is one of

Penang Hill's principal attractions. A picturesque excursion through lush tropical woods is provided by the funicular railway, which also provides sights of a variety of flora and wildlife.

A Summit: Visitors may take advantage of the pleasant temperature and experience a variety of sights at Penang Hill's peak. The historic importance of the hill is still visible thanks to the magnificent Bellevue Hotel, which was constructed during the colonial period. There are also several observation decks, eateries, and gift stores where tourists may unwind, chow down, and buy souvenirs.

Nature Walks and Trails: Penang Hill has several walking pathways and trails for nature lovers. Visitors may experience the hill's natural splendor by taking strolls or more difficult excursions. The well-kept paths provide chances to see animals, learn about tropical plants, and take in the peace of the surroundings.

Penang Botanical Gardens: The Penang Botanical Gardens, a verdant sanctuary at the base of Penang Hill, are home to a diverse range of plant species. Visitors may stroll around the gardens, take in the vibrant blossoms, and unwind in the tranquil setting. A waterfall, a lily pond, and a small zoo are also included inside the grounds.

Rooftop Walkway: The exhilarating canopy walkway experience is available at Habitat Penang Hill for those looking for an adrenaline rush. The walkway, which is suspended high in the trees, gives a unique viewpoint of the rainforest habitat and the opportunity to see the variety of local fauna.

Evening Tours: At night, Penang Hill has a distinct allure. Visitors may have a romantic supper at one of the hilltop restaurants while taking in the cool evening wind and Georgetown's glittering lights. Visitors may see the city's lit skyline from a new vantage point by taking one of the numerous night excursions.

Penang Hill provides a cool respite from the heat of the city and the opportunity to take in the splendor of nature. For lovers of nature, adventure seekers, and those looking for peace, a trip to Penang Hill guarantees a great experience whether they are taking in the breathtaking views, discovering the hill's attractions, or engaging in outdoor activities.

Penang National Park

The north-western portion of Malaysia's Penang Island is home to Penang National Park, commonly known as Taman Negara Pulau Pinang. An overview of this biodiverse national park is given below:

Environmental Diversity: Penang National Park is well known for its diverse wildlife and clean surroundings. It has a wide variety of ecological settings, including dense rainforests, mangrove swamps, sandy beaches, and rocky coasts. Numerous plant and animal species, some of which are uncommon and endangered, may be found in the park.

Hiking Routes: The national park provides possibilities for adventurers and nature lovers to discover its natural treasures on several well-maintained hiking paths that snake through the deep forest. The routes' degrees of difficulty appeals to both inexperienced hikers and casual walkers. The Canopy Walkway, Monkey Beach Trail, and Pantai Kerachut Trail are a few well-liked pathways.

Animals and Plants: A surprising variety of plant species, including enormous trees, rare orchids, and unusual ferns, may be found in Penang National Park. Wildlife watchers may see a wide range of creatures, including macaques, dusky leaf monkeys, monitor lizards, and a variety of birds. Along with sea turtles that lay their eggs on the beaches, the park is also home to the endangered Penang flying fox.

Animal Beach: Monkey Beach is one of the biggest attractions of the national park. This gorgeous beach provides a tranquil escape surrounded by thick vegetation and is accessible by boat or on foot. Sandy beaches, crystal-clear lakes, and joyful monkeys swinging among the trees are all available for visitors to unwind on.

Using a Canoe in Mangrove Forests: A guided canoe excursion may be used to explore the mangrove woods in the park, which represent a distinctive habitat. Visitors may examine the varied mangrove foliage and come across many animal species, including mudskippers, crabs, and bird species that live in the mangroves, while paddling along the peaceful waters.

Turtle Refuge: At Pantai Kerachut, a turtle sanctuary is situated inside the park. The conservation efforts being done to save sea turtles, especially the critically endangered green and olive ridley turtles, are available for visitors to learn about. Lucky visitors may even get to see young turtles being released into the ocean depending on the time of year.

Park Amenities: Picnic places, camping grounds, and other amenities are provided for visitors in Penang National Park. Additionally, there is an information center where visitors may acquire maps, discover more about the park's plants and animals, and get advice on hiking routes and other activities.

Penang National Park offers an escape into the bush and a variety of outdoor activities for nature lovers and adventure seekers as a refuge of natural beauty and biodiversity. At the core of Penang's natural heritage, this national park offers visitors an amazing experience with its different ecosystems, breathtaking scenery, and plentiful species.

Batu Ferringhi Beach

On Malaysia's Penang Island's north shore lies a well-known beach called Batu Ferringhi Beach. Batu Ferringhi Beach, which is well-known for its beautiful sandy shoreline and azure seas, provides guests with several attractions and activities. Here is a description of this well-known beach resort:

Beautiful Beaches: Batu Ferringhi Beach has immaculate sand beaches and crystal-clear waves as it runs along a scenic coastline. The beach is the ideal location for tanning, unwinding beneath the shade of palm palms, and taking in the calming murmur of the waves. Visitors may relax while admiring the natural beauty of the surroundings, walk along the coastline, or swim in the water.

Activities and Water Sports: Water sports aficionados might find paradise at Batu Ferringhi Beach. Activities available to visitors include windsurfing, parasailing, banana boat excursions, and jet skiing. The beach is a great place for snorkeling as well, letting tourists explore the nearby coral reefs and aquatic life.

Evening Market: The night market that comes to life in the evening is one of the attractions of Batu Ferringhi Beach. The market, which stretches along the main road, provides a lively environment where guests may peruse a large variety of booths offering mementos, handicrafts, apparel, accessories, and local street cuisine. It's the ideal location for shopping and enjoying Penang's delectable street cuisine.

Residences and Resorts: There are upscale resorts, boutique hotels, and inexpensive lodgings all across Batu Ferringhi Beach. Visitors may choose from a variety of choices based on their tastes and financial constraints. A lot of these places provide access to the beach, breathtaking views, and a range of facilities to improve the whole beach experience.

Hungry Hawker Stalls: Visitors may discover a plethora of hawker food booths and restaurants along the seaside promenade and in the surrounding districts, providing a broad range of delectable local and foreign cuisines. There is something for every appetite, from delectable seafood to classic Penfaresfare like Char Kway Teow and Assam Laksa.

Aromatic Garden: The Tropical Spice Garden, a verdant paradise devoted to presenting the many flora and spices of Malaysia, is located close to Batu Ferringhi and open to tourists. There are guided excursions that provide insights into the area's rich floral history and the cultural importance of spices.

Entertainment at Night: Beachfront bars, breweries, and live music venues make up the vibrant nightlife scene of Batu Ferringhi Beach. Visitors may take in the lively environment, dance to live music, or just unwind with a drink and the sea air.

Beach lovers, individuals who like participating in water sports, and those looking for a calm seaside retreat all frequent Batu Ferringhi Beach. Batu Ferringhi Beach on the alluring island of Penang offers a well-rounded beach experience with its stunning beaches, water sports, lively night market, and a variety of lodging and food choices.

Tropical Spices Park

In Teluk Bahang, a picturesque botanical park next to Batu Ferringhi Beach in Penang, Malaysia, The Tropical Spice Park is a must-see attraction. Here is a description of this unusual garden:

Diversity in Botany: The Tropical Spice Garden is a treasure trove of plant species from Malaysia and throughout the globe, covering more than 8 acres of ground. A wide variety of tropical plants, including herbs, spices, exotic trees, and medicinal plants, are on display in the garden. Discover the wonderful world of spices and herbs by exploring the garden's themed sections.

Guided tours and Spice trails: The garden provides both self-guided and guided tours, giving guests an immersive and informative experience. The many plant species, their cultural importance, culinary usage, and medicinal characteristics are all covered in detail by knowledgeable guides. Visitors may discover the history of spices, their function in commerce, and the traditional treatments linked to them.

Curry Museum: The Spice Museum, located in the Tropical Spice Garden, provides information on the history, origins, and cultural importance of spices. The museum features relics, interactive displays, and educational exhibits that trace the history of spices from their regional beginnings to their widespread usage today. Visitors may discover information on spice trade routes, conventional techniques of processing spices, and the significance of spices in many cultures.

Garden Walkways and Trails: The garden offers a quiet ambiance with its well-kept pathways and walks that wind through lush flora. The walkways are lined with a variety of vegetation, including tall trees, vibrant flowers, and fragrant herbs. Visitors may stroll along them. The garden is filled with seats and resting spots where you may unwind and enjoy the beauty of nature.

Cooking Workshops and Classes: Visitors may take culinary lessons and seminars at the Tropical Spice Garden to learn how to make traditional Malaysian cuisine using fresh herbs and spices. Participants may sample the tastes and scents of regional food while learning about Penang's culinary legacy via these hands-on activities.

Café and Gift Shop: There is a gift store in the garden where guests may buy various spices, herb mixtures, essential oils, and other botanical goods. In addition, the store sells handcrafted crafts, souvenirs, and books on gardening and spices. Additionally, there is a café on the property where guests may savor libations, snacks, and meals flavored with flavorful spices.

Unusual and Unique Occasions: Special activities held in the Tropical Spice Garden, such as cultural festivals, musical performances, and art exhibits, provide an exciting and lively environment for guests. The garden offers a distinctive setting among the grandeur of nature and is a well-liked location for weddings, private celebrations, and corporate events.

Visitors to the Tropical Spice Garden are taken on a sensory journey through the world of spices, herbs, and tropical plants. The garden provides a compelling experience that highlights the botanical legacy and cultural value of spices in Penang and beyond via its informative tours, lovely settings, culinary lessons, and cultural events.

Escape Adventureplay Theme Park

In Teluk Bahang, Penang, Malaysia, there is a thrilling outdoor adventure park called Escape Adventureplay Theme Park. Escape provides a distinctive and thrilling experience for adventurers and nature lovers of all ages. Here is a description of this daring theme park:

Adventure Sports: Theme parks like Escape Adventureplay are well known for their exciting offerings that combine adventure, physical challenge, and environment. On obstacle courses, rope courses, climbing walls, Tarzan swings, zip lines across the trees, and other tree-based activities, visitors may put their strength and agility to the test. Everybody, from novices to adrenaline addicts, will find something to enjoy at the park, which provides a range of difficulty levels.

Natural Environment: Escape Adventureplay is situated in a picturesque and relaxing atmosphere, surrounded by lush grass and natural surroundings. The park provides a distinctive setting for adventure activities since it is tucked away in a tropical jungle. It is the ideal blend of excitement and tranquility since visitors may take in the breathtaking beauty of nature while participating in heart-pounding experiences.

Treetop hikes: The canopy walkways at Escape, which let visitors see the forest from a higher vantage point, are among its best features. The tree-top paths, which are suspended high in the trees, provide expansive views of the surroundings and give visitors a close-up look at the forest environment. While admiring the grandeur of the surrounding landscape, visitors may experience the excitement of wandering amid the trees.

Aquatic Attractions: Water-based activities are also available at Escape Adventureplay to keep cool and add a dash of excitement. Visitors may ride the Tubby Racer, an inner-tube-powered water slide where riders compete on a twisting circuit. The park also has a swimming pool and a kids' water play area, offering a cool respite from the tropical heat.

Team Building Exercises: Escape Adventureplay provides corporate events and team-building programs that emphasize communication, problem-solving, and teamwork skills. To encourage cooperation and camaraderie among participants, these programs combine team-building exercises, adventure activities, and group challenges.

Kids' Playground: Monkey School, a section of the park designated for younger guests, offers interactive games and age-appropriate adventure activities. In a secure and supervised setting, the space is intended to foster children's creativity, physical development, and problem-solving skills.

Environmental Awareness: Theme park Escape Adventureplay encourages environmentally conscious behavior. The park places a strong emphasis on the value of protecting the environment and informs visitors about regional ecology and conservation initiatives. Additionally, it uses eco-friendly techniques in its operations, such as recycling and trash reduction.

Theme park Escape Adventureplay provides an exhilarating journey in a breathtaking natural environment. The park offers a wonderful experience for individuals, families, and groups searching for an exhilarating outdoor adventure in Penang thanks to its broad choice of adventure activities, picturesque surroundings, and dedication to environmental conscience.

VI. TASTING PENANG'S CULINARY DELIGHTS

1. Penang Hawker Cuisine.

Penang is known for being a gastronomic haven, especially for its delectable hawker fare. The island is home to several hawker foods stands that provide a broad range of mouth watering delicacies at reasonable prices that capture the unique tastes of Penang's cosmopolitan background. The following delicacies from Penang's famous hawker centers may tempt your palate:

Tofu: Char Kway Teow You must taste this stir-fried noodle dish when visiting Penang. This dish often consists of flat rice noodles, shrimp, cockles, bean sprouts, Chinese sausage, and eggs that have all been stir-fried in a tasty sauce that blends sweet, salty, and a little bit of heat.

Assam Laksa: A tangy and hot noodle soup called Assam Laksa is made with rice noodles, fish broth, tamarind, chili, and a variety of herbs and vegetables. The fragrant and acidic broth, which is often produced from mackerel or sardines, is what gives the dish its distinctive taste.

Mee Hokkien: With prawns, pork pieces, bean sprouts, and a hearty black soy sauce, Hokkien Mee is a meal made of thick yellow noodles and rice vermicelli. A fragrant broth is used to boil the noodles, giving them a delicious flavor and scent.

Curry Mee: Curry Mee is a kind of noodle soup that has a flavorful and hot curry broth. Typically, it includes rice vermicelli or yellow noodles, cockles, tofu puffs, and a variety of garnishes such as bean sprouts, cuttlefish, and mint leaves. A combination of spices, coconut milk, and chili paste is used to make the curry broth.

Rojak: A variety of fruits and vegetables, including cucumbers, pineapples, bean sprouts, and jicama, are combined in the distinctive and savory salad known as rojak, which is then dressed with a tangy shrimp paste dressing. Crushed peanuts and crisp fritters are often used as garnishes to offer additional texture.

Nasi Kandar: Popular Malaysian cuisine Nasi Kandar was created in Penang. You may mix and match the side dishes and curries that come with the steamed rice to create your ideal dinner. There are several options available, including fried chicken, seafood, veggies, and hot curries.

Apam Balik: A delicious pancake from Malaysia called apam balik is formed with a batter of flour, sugar, eggs, and coconut milk. Usually fried in a circular pan, it has a sweet filling made of crushed peanuts, sugar, and sometimes sweet corn. The pancake is soft and fluffy inside and crisp on the exterior when folded into a half-moon shape.

Cendol: A dessert called cendol is made of jelly noodles with pandan flavor, coconut milk, shaved ice, and palm sugar syrup. Red beans are often used as a topping, and sometimes glutinous rice or sweet corn as well. On a hot day, cendol is a common treat to cool down.

These are just a handful of Penang's mouthwatering hawker fare attractions. The many tastes and culinary pleasures of Penang's hawker food scene are guaranteed to satiate any food lover's needs, from savory noodles and spicy curries to sweet desserts and refreshing beverages.

2. Famous Penang Street Food

Penang is renowned for its thriving street food scene, which serves a broad variety of delicious delicacies that are adored by both residents and visitors. You shouldn't miss any of these popular Penang street food specialties:

Penang Char Kway Teow: Using flat rice noodles, cockles, bean sprouts, Chinese sausage, eggs, and a savory soy sauce, char kway teow is a stir-fried noodle dish. As a result of being cooked in a hot wok, it has a smoky, somewhat burnt taste.

Penang Hokkien Mee: The Hokkien Mee served in Penang is distinct from that served in other cities. prawns, pork pieces, bean sprouts, and a dark soy sauce are stir-fried with yellow noodles and rice vermicelli in this dish. Sambal chili paste is often offered on the side with the entrée.

Penyajak: An assortment of fruits and vegetables, including cucumber, pineapple, jicama, and bean sprouts, are combined in the well-known Malaysian salad known as rojak. Crushed peanuts are used as a garnish and to provide texture to the sweet and sour shrimp paste sauce.

Murtabak Penang: A thin layer of dough is used to make the pancake-like murtabak, which is packed with ground beef, onions, and spices. The curry sauce is often provided on the side for dipping.

Here are just a few classic Penang street food delicacies to get you started. The island is a foodie's heaven, and you may find even more delectable culinary treats by strolling through the busy hawker booths and food markets.

Nyonya Cuisine

The distinctive and tasty Nyonya cuisine, commonly referred to as Peranakan or Straits Chinese cuisine, mixes Chinese, Malay, and Indonesian elements. It developed as a result of intermarrying Malay and Indonesian locals with Chinese immigrants in the old Straits Settlements, which included Penang. The complex tastes, brilliant colors, and wide variety of dishes that make up Nyonya cuisine are well-known. Following are some salient characteristics and well-known Nyonya dishes:

Combination of Flavors: Nyonya cuisine mixes Chinese cooking methods and ingredients with the flavorful, spiciness, and scent of Malay and Indonesian ingredients. It uses aromatic herbs and spices including lemongrass, galangal, turmeric, belacan (shrimp paste), and tamarind in addition to a balance of sweet, sour, and savory tastes.

Signature Recipes: Using fermented soybean paste and palm sugar to make a thick sauce, ayam pongteh is a dish of slow-cooked chicken and potatoes.

- Otak-Otak: A grilled dish made of spiced fish paste wrapped in banana leaves that has a smokey, aromatic taste.

- Nyonya Laksa is a spicy curry noodle soup made with coconut milk that is garnished with prawns, fish cakes, tofu puffs, and bean sprouts.

- A pork stew like Ayam Pongteh but made with pork rather than chicken.

- A spicily sour soup cooked with fish guts, vegetables, and tamarind juice is known as Perut Ikan.

- Crispy pastry cups known as "Kueh Pie Tee" are stuffed with a combination of prawns, shredded veggies, and a sweet and sour sauce.

- A thick and flavorful chicken curry made with a variety of spices and coconut milk is called kari kapitan.

- Itik Tim is a transparent soup that is created with salted vegetables, duck, and a variety of herbs and spices.

Employing Belacan: An essential component of Nyonya cuisine is belacan, a fermented shrimp paste. It gives food a distinctive umami taste and scent. Before being added to different sauces, curries, and sambal chili pastes, it is often roasted or fried.

Traditional Methods of Cooking: Traditional cooking methods used in Nyonya cuisines, such as braising, stewing, and slow cooking, are used to infuse flavors into meals and produce soft meats. For added depth and complexity, it also uses sophisticated spice pastes, which are created by blending a variety of fresh ingredients.

Complex Desserts: Kueh, a kind of delicacy popular in Nyonya, is renowned for its delicate taste and brilliant colors. Ingredients including glutinous rice, coconut milk, palm sugar, and pandan leaves are often used to make these bite-sized delights. Popular Nyonya kueh include the pandan crepes filled with coconut known as kueh dadar, the tiered rice cake known as kueh lapis, and the tapioca cake known as kueh bengka.

The mix of Chinese and Malay tastes that results in Nyonya cuisine create a lively and distinctive culinary legacy. A lovely way to enjoy the rich cultural and culinary traditions of the Peranakan population is to sample the many Nyonya delicacies available in Penang

Seafood Restaurants

Penang is known for its tasty and fresh seafood, and the island has a variety of seafood eateries to suit all tastes and price ranges. Here are several well-liked seafood restaurants in Penang, whether you're searching for a casual eating setting by the water or a formal dining venue that specializes in seafood specialties:

Hawker Center on Gurney Drive: Popular outdoor food court Gurney Drive Hawker Center serves a wide variety of seafood specialties. You may find kiosks selling seafood-based noodles and soups, as well as grilled fish, prawns, clams, and crab. It's a terrific location to take in the lively scene and enjoy a variety of regional seafood treats.

Restaurant Ocean Green Seafood: Ocean Green Seafood Restaurant, which is situated in Batu Ferringhi, is well-known for its fresh seafood and breathtaking beachfront environment. A variety of foods cooked in different cooking methods are available at the restaurant, including steamed, grilled, stir-fried, and hot chili dishes. Butter prawns, black pepper crab, and steamed fish are a few things you must try.

Ferringhi Garden Dining Room: In Batu Ferringhi, there is a classy and charming restaurant called Ferringhi Garden Restaurant. The restaurant offers a delicious selection of seafood selections, such as grilled lobster, seafood spaghetti, fish and chips, and seafood platters, in addition to its gorgeous garden setting. It's the perfect option for a memorable dining experience or a special event.

Seafood Village at Crab Village: Tanjung Tokong's Crab Village Seafood Village is well-known for its crab-based cuisine. The restaurant showcases the adaptability of this seafood delicacy by serving a range of crab recipes, including chili crab, butter crab, and salted egg yolk crab. There are also other seafood selections including fish, clams, and prawns.

Seafood Paradise on the Water: At Tambun Seafood Village, there is a unique seafood dining experience called Floating Seafood Paradise. The eatery is made up of floating bungalows on a lake where you can unwind and indulge in a seafood feast. A variety of fresh seafood, cooked to your liking, including fish, prawns, crabs, and shellfish, may be found on the menu.

Cafe at Sea Pearl Lagoon: In Teluk Bahang, the Sea Pearl Lagoon Cafe provides a relaxed setting and cuisine bursting with mouthwatering seafood specialties. While savoring delicious fares like butter calamari, sweet and sour fish, spicy prawns, and steamed fish, you can take in the beautiful scenery around you.

These are only a few examples of seafood establishments in Penang. The island is well-known for its plentiful seafood choices, so trying out several restaurants will let you sample a broad range of tastes and styles.

Traditional Snacks and Desserts

Penang is renowned for having a diverse range of traditional sweets and snacks that are enjoyed by both residents and tourists. The various influences prevalent on the island are often reflected in these sweet snacks and desserts. Here are some well-liked local treats and nibbles to sample in Penang:

- **Kueh**: In Penang, the term "kueh" describes a variety of little traditional cakes and snacks. These vibrant and tasty sweets are produced using glutinous rice, coconut milk, palm sugar, and pandan leaves as components. Kueh Dadar (pandan crepes stuffed with coconut), Kueh Bingka (tapioca cake), and Kueh Lapis (layered rice cake) are some of the most well-known kueh types.

- **Apom:** A popular traditional snack called apom is prepared from fermented rice batter. It is prepared on a unique spherical pan to give it the appearance of a thin, crispy pancake. Apom is a delicious snack to eat throughout the day and is often served with a sweet coconut or banana filling.

- **Pneah Tau Sar:** Tambun Biscuits, commonly referred to as Tau Sar Pneah, is a well-known Penang treat. A flaky pastry shell encases a sweet and aromatic mung bean paste in these pastries. They make a terrific culinary keepsake from Penang and are often eaten with a cup of Chinese tea.

- **Kacang Ice:** Shaved ice desserts like Ice Kacang, also known as ABC (Ais Batu Campur), are popular in Penang. It has a mountain of finely shaved ice on top of which are a variety of vibrant toppings, including red beans, sweet corn, jelly cubes, grass jelly, and syrup. Condensed milk is sometimes poured on top for sweetness.

- **Cendol**: Penang residents love the iconic Malaysian delicacy called cendol. Jelly noodles with pandan flavor, coconut milk, shaved ice, and palm sugar syrup are the main ingredients. It is a great way to cool yourself on a hot day and is often topped with red beans for additional texture.

- **Kuih Muih:** A variety of traditional Malay kueh, or snacks, are referred to as kuih muih. These tasty morsels are available in a variety of sizes, hues, and tastes. Kuih Ketayap (pandan crepes with coconut filling), Kuih Talam (pandan and coconut custard), and Kuih Karas (deep-fried sweet potato balls) are a few delectable examples.

- **The Pisang Goreng:** In Penang, deep-fried bananas are known as pisang goreng. Ripe bananas are battered and deep-fried till crisp and golden. Both residents and tourists delight in it, particularly when accompanied by a nice cup of tea or coffee.

You may discover a variety of traditional sweets and nibbles in Penang, just to name a few. Discovering the neighborhood markets, food carts, and bakeries will introduce you to a world of delicious sweets and snacks that highlight the area's long culinary traditions.

TOP 5 Restaurants to Eat

Line Clear Nasi Kandar:
Line Clear Nasi Kandar, a renowned establishment with a location in George Town, is well-known for its tasty and genuine nasi kandar. Steamed rice is served with a variety of curries, meats, and veggies in this classic Malaysian cuisine. Since 1947, Line Clear Nasi Kandar has been serving up mouthwatering nasi kandar. It is especially well known for its flavorful and creamy gravies.

Red Garden Night Market & Food Paradise:
Along Jalan Penang lies Red Garden Food Paradise, a popular open-air food court that serves a wide variety of regional and international cuisine. Popular Malaysian foods including char kway teow, satay, laksa, and others are available at these vendors. It's a terrific location to experience

various meals in a bright and energetic setting.

Tek Sen Restaurant

George Town's Tek Sen Restaurant is well known for serving delicious genuine Chinese Thai food. Due to its delectable meals made with fresh ingredients and old-fashioned traditions, the restaurant has developed a devoted following. Numerous stir-fried meals, hot and sour soups, and clay pot delicacies are offered on the menu. Both the fried tofu and the crispy roast pork come highly recommended.

Mews Café:

Mews Café in George Town provides customers with a warm and inviting atmosphere since it is housed in a gorgeously renovated historic structure. Modern fusion cuisine with an emphasis on regional ingredients is the café's specialty. Mews Café provides an enjoyable eating experience with robust breakfast selections, delicious main dishes, and mouthwatering desserts. Banana fritters and Hainanese chicken chops are popular dishes.

Feringgi Grill:
The upmarket restaurant Feringgi Grill is housed inside Shangri-La's Rasa Sayang Resort & Spa in Batu Ferringhi. It provides great meals and a breathtaking seaside view. It is well known for its exquisite service, top-quality steaks, and fresh seafood. A restaurant is a great option for a special event or romantic supper because of its extensive menu of foreign and Western cuisine and cozy setting.

These top five restaurants in Penang provide a range of eating options, from fine dining to fusion food to traditional Malaysian treats. These eateries will please your palate and provide you with a lasting impression of Penang's cuisine, whether you're looking for traditional street food or a fine dining experience.

VII. DAY TRIPS FROM PENANG

While Penang itself has a wide range of sights and activities, the surrounding area also has several alluring places that are ideal for day visits. There are many places to visit outside of Penang, including lovely islands, historic cities, and natural and cultural attractions. This chapter will walk you through some of the greatest day excursions you can take from Penang, giving you thorough descriptions of each place and what to anticipate there.

Langkawi:
Langkawi, an archipelago of 99 islands famed for its immaculate beaches, lush jungles, and duty-free shopping, is just a short boat ride or flight from Penang. Spend the day discovering Langkawi's amazing natural beauty. For breathtaking views, take a cable car trip to Mount Cincang or stroll

over the curving Langkawi Sky Bridge. Take part in water activities, explore Underwater World Langkawi, or just unwind on Pantai Cenang's fine beaches.

Cameron Highlands:
Enter the cool and refreshing Cameron Highlands to escape the sweltering heat of Penang. This hill resort, well-known for its tea estates, strawberry fields, and beautiful surroundings, provides a peaceful refuge. Explore the vibrant flower gardens, stop by the renowned BOH Tea Plantation, take a leisurely walk around the tea plantations, and taste some fresh strawberries at the farms. For a closer look at the area's distinctive flora and wildlife, don't miss a trip to the Mossy Forest and the famed Butterfly Farm.

Penang Mainland:
You may discover lovely towns and historical landmarks by crossing over to the Penang mainland. Visit Bukit Mertajam,

which is well-known for the surrounding Bukit Mertajam Recreational Forest and the historic St. Anne's Church. Explore the Tow Boo Kong Temple and wander along the picturesque Butterworth Art Walk in the ancient town of Butterworth. Visit Balik Pulau and take in the picturesque villages, paddy fields, and fruit orchards for a flavor of traditional village life.

Ken Lok Si Temple and Penang Hill:
Penang Hill is a well-known destination inside Penang, but a day trip to this hill town and the surrounding Kek Lok Si Temple is strongly advised. Take the funicular train up to Penang Hill to take in the expansive island vistas and the refreshing mountain air. Visit Kek Lok Si Temple next; it is Southeast Asia's biggest Buddhist temple. Admire the complex architecture, go around the different halls and pagodas, and be sure to see the magnificent statue of the Goddess of Mercy.

Ipoh:
If you go further, the city of Ipoh provides a unique mix of culture, tradition, and mouthwatering cuisine. Discover the picturesque Old Town, which is renowned for its colorful street art and colonial architecture. Experience Ipoh's world-famous culinary treats like bean sprout chicken, salt-baked chicken, and white coffee. Marvel at the spectacular architecture of the Ipoh Railway Station. Visit the amazing cave temples like Sam Poh Tong and Kek Lok Tong.

You may explore the variety of activities and experiences offered in the area by leaving Penang on day excursions. Each day excursion offers distinctive discoveries and unforgettable experiences, from the island beauty of Langkawi to the cold mountains of Cameron mountains and the historical charm of Ipoh. So make time on your trip to Penang to discover these hidden beauties and broaden your travel horizons.

VIII. PRACTICAL INFORMATION AND TIPS

Useful Phrases

➢ Hello: Salam (sah-lam)

➢ Good morning: Selamat pagi (seh-lah-mat pah-gee)

➢ Good afternoon: Selamat tengah hari (seh-lah-mat ten-gah ha-ree)

➢ Good evening: Selamat petang (seh-lah-mat peh-tang)

➢ Good night: Selamat malam (sch-lah-mat ma-lam)

➢ Thank you: Terima kasih (teh-ree-mah kah-see)

➢ You're welcome: Sama-sama (sah-mah sah-mah)

➢ Yes: Ya (yah)

➢ No: Tidak (tee-dahk)

➢ Excuse me: Maaf (mah-af)

➢ Sorry: Maafkan saya (mah-af-kan sah-ya)

➢ I don't understand: Saya tidak faham (sah-ya tee-dahk fah-ham)

- Do you speak English?: Boleh cakap Bahasa Inggeris? (boh-leh chah-kap bah-ha-sah ing-geris?)
- Where is...?: Di mana...? (dee mah-nah)
- How much is this?: Berapa harga ini? (be-rah-pah har-gah ee-nee)
- I would like...: Saya mahu... (sah-ya mah-hoo)
- Can you help me?: Boleh tolong saya? (boh-leh toh-long sah-ya)

- What is your name?: Siapa nama anda? (see-ah-pah nah-mah ahn-dah)
- My name is...: Nama saya... (nah-mah sah-ya)
- I'm sorry, I don't speak Malay well: Maaf, saya tidak fasih berbahasa Melayu (mah-af, sah-ya tee-dahk fah-seeh ber-bah-ha-sah meh-lay-yoo)

Enjoy interactions and have a wonderful time in Penang!

Helpful Contacts and Websites

Emergency Services:

Police: 999

Fire and Rescue: 994

Ambulance: 999

Tourism Hotline:

Tourism Malaysia Hotline: 1-300-88-5050

Penang Tourist Information Centers:

Penang Global Tourism: +604-264 3494 / +604-262 0202

Penang State Tourism Development, Arts, Culture, and Heritage (PETACH): +604-650 5133 / +604-650 5136

Penang International Airport:

General Enquiries: +604-643 4411

Flight Information: +604-643 4412

Transportation:

Rapid Penang (Public Bus Service): +604-238 1212

Penang Port (Ferry Service): +604-210 5000

Hospitals and Medical Assistance:

Penang General Hospital: +604-222 5333

Gleneagles Penang Medical Centre: +604-222 9111

Mount Miriam Cancer Hospital: +604-892 3888

Tourism Websites:

Penang Global Tourism: www.visitpenang.gov.my

Penang State Tourism Development, Arts, Culture, and Heritage (PETACH):

www.penangtourism.my

Transportation Apps:

Grab (Ride-hailing service):

www.grab.com

MyCar (Ride-hailing service):

www.mycar2u.com.my

Weather Updates:

Malaysian Meteorological Department:

www.met.gov.my

Embassy Contacts:

Contact information for the embassy of your country in Malaysia is available through the diplomatic or foreign affairs office of your nation.

Keeping these contacts on your phone or having them on hand when visiting Penang is usually a smart idea. They can help you in an emergency, provide you with information, and give you advice while you're there. Don't forget to research local rules and laws about safety and travel before your trip.

Security And Safety Tips

It's crucial to put your safety and well-being first while visiting any place, especially Penang. Following are some security and safety recommendations for your trip:

- Research the current safety situation in Penang before your trip, and keep up with any cautions or warnings issued by the foreign affairs office of your nation. To guarantee a straightforward and secure experience, familiarize yourself with regional laws, traditions, and regulations.

- Protect your possessions: At all times, keep your valuables, such as passports, cash, and devices, safe. Store your valuables in a hotel safe or a secured locker. To keep your cash and important papers secure when exploring, avoid carrying huge quantities of cash and think about wearing a money belt or utilizing a concealed bag.

- Be careful with your personal belongings: Pay close attention to them while you're in public areas like marketplaces, congested streets, and transit. Keep an eye out for pickpockets and stay away from bright jewelry or pricey goods that can draw unwelcome attention.

- Stay at a respected hotel: Pick hotels that have a solid reputation for safety and security and positive reviews. Verify the presence of adequate security measures, such as surveillance cameras, secure entrances, and well-lit common areas, at the hotel or guesthouse.

- Use dependable modes of transportation: Select authorized

taxis, ride-hailing apps, or trustworthy automobile rental businesses. Be mindful of your surroundings and keep a watch on your valuables while using public transit. Avoid going alone at night, particularly in remote or unknown regions.

- Be vigilant of tourist-targeted fraud and scams, such as overcharging, phony tour operators, and deals that appear too good to be true. Only reserve trips and activities from trustworthy travel companies or reliable sources.

- Respect local laws and traditions by being knowledgeable about Penang's traditions, laws, and customs. Respect local sensitivity, cultural customs, and religious locations. When visiting religious places, dress modestly and abide by any rules or dress regulations that may be in place.

- Make sure you have a dependable way to stay in touch, such as a local SIM card or a working mobile phone with roaming capability. Give a family member or acquaintance you can trust a copy of your itinerary, and keep in touch with them while you're away.

- Always follow your gut feelings: If you ever feel uneasy or dangerous in a situation, follow your gut feelings and leave. Stick to densely inhabited and well-lit locations and stay away from lonely regions, particularly at night.

- Travel insurance: Take into account acquiring travel insurance that covers personal items, trip cancellations, and medical emergencies. To understand the coverage and processes for filing a claim, thoroughly read the policy.

- Personal safety should always come first while traveling. You may have a safe and pleasurable time seeing Penang's stunning sites by being vigilant, following the appropriate safety measures, and being aware of your surroundings.

Medical and Health Facilities

In case of any unanticipated problems, it's important to know about health and medical services while visiting Penang. Here are some crucial specifics of Penang's medical and health systems:

- General Healthcare: Hospitals, clinics, and medical facilities are only a few of the general healthcare options available in Penang. Among the prominent choices are:

- Penang General Hospital (Hospital Pulau Pinang), a significant public hospital offering a range of medical services, is situated in Georgetown. Phone number: +604-222-5333.

- Private hospital with extensive medical services: Gleneagles Penang Medical Centre. Phone number: +604-222 9111.

- The private hospital noted for its specialized services and medical knowledge: Adventist Hospital Penang. Call us at +604-222-7200.

- International Clinics: Several clinics in Penang treat patients from across the world and provide a broad variety of medical services. These clinics often feature staff members who understand English and provide high-quality medical services.

Examples include:

- Island Hospital is a private healthcare facility that provides a full range of medical services. Call us at +604-228-8222.

- a private medical facility with a range of specializations and services called Loh Guan Lye Specialist Centre. Call us at +604-238-8888.

- Travel health and immunizations: It is recommended that you speak with a healthcare provider or travel clinic before your journey to Penang to go through any necessary vaccinations or health precautions related to your travel agenda. They may provide information on suggested vaccinations, malaria prevention (if necessary), and other travel health recommendations.

- Pharmacy: There are several pharmacies in Penang where you may get over-the-counter medicines, cosmetics, and essential medical supplies. Look for pharmacies that are close to hospitals, supermarkets, or shopping centers. Always make sure you have your prescription pills on hand and in their original containers.

- Insurance Coverage: It is highly advised that you get travel insurance that includes emergency medical coverage. Examine your insurance to learn more about the specifics of the medical costs, evacuation, and repatriation coverage.

- Emergency Services: Dial 999 to reach your neighborhood's emergency services in the event of a medical emergency.

It's crucial to remember that healthcare services might be expensive, so be ready to pay for medical care and services. Keep vital contact information, such as hospital locations and phone numbers, with you at all times so you can easily access it.

Before visiting Penang, it is also a good idea to review the most recent travel warnings and health advice issued by the World Health Organization (WHO) or the foreign affairs office of your nation to be aware of any current health issues or prerequisites.

Prioritize your health and well-being during your journey by maintaining excellent cleanliness, drinking enough water, and taking the required safety measures to avoid any health problems.

Customs and Etiquettes

To have a great and culturally aware experience when visiting Penang, it's crucial to follow the local traditions and etiquette. Here are some important traditions and manners to remember:

- Dress code: It is polite to wear modest clothing while entering places of worship or more conservative neighborhoods. It is advisable to cover the shoulders and knees for both men and women. Due to the tropical temperature, it is best to dress comfortably and simply.

- Malaysians often shake hands and smile when they shake someone's hand. It is considered acceptable to address someone using courtesy titles, such as "Encik" for Mr., "Cik" for Miss, and "Puan" for Mrs. Additionally, it's traditional to shake hands or give and receive something with the right hand.

- Malaysia is a cosmopolitan nation with a wide range of races and faiths. Avoid making disparaging remarks or acting offensively to show respect for all cultures and beliefs. Be sensitive to regional traditions and sensibilities, especially at places of worship and during religious holidays.

- Shoes: It is usual to take off your shoes while entering houses, places of worship, or certain other businesses. To decide if it is required, look for signs like a shoe rack or other individuals taking off their shoes.

- Food Etiquette: Use your right hand while eating with your hands, as is customary for several regional foods. The left hand is seen as impure. It is polite to hold off on starting to eat until the host or the oldest person has done so. Avoid pointing or manipulating your food with your chopsticks.

- Respect for Elders: Respect for elders is highly regarded in Malaysian society. When speaking to elderly people, use respectful pronouns like "Uncle" or "Auntie," followed by their name or title. Offering your seat to an old person or someone in need is also considered nice.

- Public Conduct: Retain a degree of humility and refrain from public shows of love since these actions could be seen as impolite in Malaysian culture. When speaking in public, be cautious of your loudness and abstain from offensive or disruptive conduct.

- Tipping: Since a 10% service fee is often included in restaurant and hotel bills, tipping is not customary in Malaysia. However, if the service was very good, a modest tip would be welcomed.

- When taking a photograph of someone, particularly in more private or intimate situations, always get their consent. Respect any warnings or restrictions on photographing at tourist attractions, places of worship, or on private property.

Although English is frequently spoken, particularly in tourist regions, it is welcomed if you can learn a few simple Malay greetings to indicate that you are interested in the culture of the country. Malaysians often recognize the effort and may react more affably. Always have an open mind and be eager to learn and adapt while engaging in new cultural experiences.

IX. TRAVELING IN PENANG WITH KIDS

The entire family may have a wonderful and delightful time traveling with kids in Penang. Here are some pointers and ideas to make sure a vacation is easygoing and family-friendly:

- **Select a Family-Friendly Hotel:** Look for hotels that welcome families with young children. Think about lodgings or resorts with features like playgrounds, swimming pools, or kids' clubs. More space and convenience may be offered via family suites or connected rooms.

- **Plan family-friendly activities**: There are several family-friendly attractions in Penang. Include exciting, age-appropriate activities like going to interactive museums, touring theme parks, or going on outdoor excursions. The Penang Butterfly Farm, ESCAPE Adventureplay Theme Park, and Penang Toy Museum are a few well-liked kid-friendly attractions.

- **Visit the Beaches:** The lovely beaches in Penang, such as Batu Ferringhi, provide chances for family enjoyment. Spend the day swimming, playing in the water, or making sandcastles. When traveling with small children in particular, keep safety in mind and choose beaches that have lifeguards on duty.

- **Explore Nature:** Take your kids to Penang National Park so they may hike around the park, see animals, and have a picnic among the beautiful vegetation. Another excellent place to teach youngsters about the local flora and wildlife is the Tropical Spice Garden.

- **Food choices:** Penang is renowned for its delectable cuisine, but it's important to take your children's dietary requirements and tastes into account. Find eateries or hawker centers that welcome kids and provide a range of selections, including well-known cuisine. High chairs and kid-friendly meals are available at certain establishments.

- Keep Your Children Hydrated by Carrying Water Bottles and Encouraging Regular Drinking: Penang's tropical environment may be hot and humid, so make sure your children keep hydrated by carrying water bottles. To shield their skin from the sun's rays, use sunscreen, and outfit them in breathable, light clothing.

- Keep a watch on your kids at all times, particularly in busy places or when they are close to water. Make sure they are aware of the fundamental safety procedures, and decide on a meeting place in case anybody becomes separated. Learn the local hospitals' phone numbers and emergency contact information.

- Be Aware of Cultural Differences: Inform your kids about Penang's unique traditions and cultural sensitivity. Remind children to observe any restrictions or dress standards in such areas and to show respect while visiting religious sites.

- Plan for Rest and pauses: Taking a trip with kids may be exhausting; thus, organizing frequent pauses so that they can refresh. Plan shorter excursions that allow you plenty of downtimes and unstructured play.

- Carry the essentials, like additional clothing, food, wet wipes, and hand sanitizers. Pack diapers, baby food, and any other necessities your younger children may need.

Keep in mind that every kid is unique, so adjust your ideas and activities to fit their ages, interests, and levels of energy. When traveling with children, flexibility and patience are essential, so be ready to modify your plans and take pauses as necessary. Making enduring family experiences while exploring Penang with your kids is possible with the right planning and forethought.

X. IDEAL PENANG ITINERARIES

Day 1:

- Explore the Georgetown Heritage Area in the morning. Visit well-known sites including the Kek Lok Si Temple, the Cheong Fatt Tze Mansion, and the Khoo Kongsi Clan House.

- Enjoy a street art tour around Georgetown in the afternoon. Visit Armenian Street to see the vibrant murals and one-of-a-kind street artworks.

- During the evening, take in the lively ambiance of Batu Ferringhi Night Market. Take a stroll around the market, buy some trinkets, and eat some delectable street cuisine.

Day 2:

- Early in the morning, visit Penang Hill. Take the funicular up to the summit for sweeping views of the island. Visit places like Habitat Penang Hill and the Owl Museum.

- Visit the Penang National Park in the afternoon. To see animals, go on a nature trek, a boat trip, or a stroll to Monkey Beach.

- Explore the busy Gurney Drive neighborhood in the evening. Visit Gurney Plaza to shop, eat at nearby restaurants, and take in the lively ambiance.

Day 3:

- Visit the tropical spice garden in the morning. Learn about the numerous plants and spices that can be found in the area by taking a guided tour.

- Discover Little India's diverse cultural heritage in the afternoon. Visit the Sri Mahamariamman Temple, stroll through the energetic streets, and savor some delectable Indian food.

- Evening: At Straits Quay Marina Mall, enjoy a tranquil sunset. Discover the waterfront promenade, enjoy meals at waterfront eateries, and attend live music events.

Itinerary for Families (4 Days):

Day 1:

- Visit the Penang Interactive 3D Museum in the morning. Enjoy engaging art displays and have fun with your photography.

- Explore the Penang Butterfly Farm in the afternoon. Explore diverse butterfly species, stroll around the butterfly enclosure, and get knowledge about the butterfly life cycle.

- Head to Batu Ferringhi Beach in the evening. Allow the youngsters to play in the sand, swim, and engage in other beach-related activities.

Day 2:

- Spend the day at the ESCAPE Adventureplay Theme Park in the morning. Experience exhilarating rides, challenging obstacle courses, and fun family activities.

- Visit the Penang Toy Museum in the afternoon. Enjoy your memories while admiring the vast collection of toys from all around the globe.

- Evening: Enjoy a stroll along Georgetown's Clan Jetties as dusk falls. Enjoy the adorable stilted wooden homes and take lovely pictures.

Day 3:

- Visit the Penang State Museum and Art Gallery in the morning. Learn about Penang's history and cultural heritage by exploring the exhibitions.

- Afternoon: Spend the day having a blast in the indoor play area known as Adventure Zone. Give the youngsters access to a variety of play areas and engaging activities.

- Take a leisurely trishaw ride around Georgetown in the evening. Take in the views, sounds, and history of the city while riding on a trishaw.

Day 4:

- Explore the Penang Avatar Secret Garden in the morning. As you meander around the lit garden, marvel at the amazing light shows.

- Visit the Penang Time Tunnel in the afternoon. A trip through Penang's history may be experienced via interactive exhibits and displays.

- Evening: Enjoy a hawker food extravaganza in a busy food court. Let the youngsters sample various regional cuisines and tastes.

These itineraries enable you to make the most of your stay in Penang while catering to various interests and preferences. They include cultural discovery, outdoor pursuits, and family-friendly sites. You are welcome to alter the itineraries to suit your requirements and interests.

XI. CONCLUSION

In summary, Penang is a fascinating location that provides a fusion of fascinating culture, breathtaking natural beauty, and mouthwatering food. Penang has something for everyone, whether you want to explore the UNESCO-designated Georgetown Heritage Area, go on exhilarating experiences at theme parks, or just unwind on the stunning beaches.

To help you make the most of your trip, we've examined Penang's must-see attractions as well as its lesser-known attractions in this travel guide.

You have now experienced the wide range of captivating sights that genuinely distinguish Penang, from well-known sites like the Khoo Kongsi Clan House and Kek Lok Si Temple to lesser-known gems like the Armenian Street Park and Hin Bus Depot Art Centre.

Additionally, the practical components of your trip have been addressed in the book, such as lodging alternatives, transit options, visa needs, currency and money concerns, and advice on remaining safe and healthy. We have also looked into regional traditions and etiquette to help you traverse Penang's diverse cultural environment with respect and understanding.

The gastronomic wonders of Penang, with its renowned hawker food booths and lively street food scene, are indescribable. Your taste buds are in for a treat as you enjoy the tastes of this culinary paradise, from delectable meals like Char Kway Teow and Assam Laksa to traditional sweets and snacks.

Every kind of visitor may find something to enjoy in Penang, whether they are alone, traveling with companions, or traveling with kids.

The offered itineraries may be altered to fit your tastes and interests, guaranteeing a memorable and satisfying experience.

Take the time to immerse yourself in Penang's rich history, engage with the welcoming inhabitants, and enjoy the distinctive cultural mosaic that makes this place so remarkable as you travel throughout Penang. Penang will make a deep effect on your heart and mind—from meandering through the streets decorated with colorful street art to taking in the architectural marvels and natural scenery.

Take with you the memories, encounters, and fresh appreciation for this amazing place as you say goodbye to Penang. We hope that our travel manual has been an invaluable travel companion, giving you the information and motivation you need to make the most of your stay in Penang.

As you start your voyage in Penang, the Pearl of the Orient, may your travels be full of pleasure, discovery, and moments of amazement.

Penang's Dos and Don'ts

Tips for Penang:

- Do sample the local cuisine: Char Kway Teow, Nasi Kandar, and Penang Laksa are among Penang's most well-known delicacies.

- Do take the time to visit Georgetown Heritage Area: Stroll around the city's ancient streets, take in the colonial architecture and take in the colorful street art.

- Do explore the historical and cultural sites: To fully experience Penang's rich cultural legacy, visit places like the St.

George's Church, Kek Lok Si Temple, and Khoo Kongsi Clan House.

- Do bargain in the markets: Feel free to haggle over costs while shopping at establishments like Batu Ferringhi Night Market to get the greatest offers on trinkets, apparel, and handicrafts.

- Respect local traditions and customs by keeping in mind Penang's cultural standards. before visiting religious places, dress modestly, take off your shoes before entering temples, and be friendly to locals.

Penang don'ts:

- Do not litter: Penang takes pride in its cleanliness, so do your part to preserve the environment by properly disposing of your rubbish.

- To ensure both your safety and the protection of the animals you see when visiting locations like Penang National Park, keep your distance from them and refrain from touching or otherwise upsetting them.

- Respect religious sites: When visiting mosques or temples, act with decency, adhere to any clothing regulations, and refrain from snapping photographs in off-limits areas.

- Drink bottled or filtered water instead of tap water to prevent any possible health hazards. Take a reusable water bottle with you and fill it up with trustworthy sources.

- Avoid participation in unlawful activities, such as dealing in illicit substances or using illegal drugs, as you would in any place. To guarantee a secure and pleasurable stay, familiarize yourself with the rules and ordinances in the area.

You may travel throughout Penang with respect for the people, place, and traditions by adhering to these dos and don'ts. Having fun while being a responsible and ethical tourist, enjoy your stay in Penang.

Penang FAQs

What time of year is ideal for visiting Penang?
A: The dry season, which normally lasts between December and February, is the ideal time to visit Penang. With less humidity and rain, the weather is often nice. Penang, however, is accessible all year round; the monsoon season lasts from September to November.

How can I get to Penang?
A: You may go to Penang via boat, road, and air. Both local and international flights are

served by the Penang International Airport. If you'd rather use the road, you may get to Penang by bus or automobile via the Butterworth-Penang Bridge or the ferry service. Additionally, there are rail connections to Butterworth, which serves as Penang's mainland entry point.

What kind of currency is used in Penang?
A: The Malaysian Ringgit (MYR) is the official currency of Penang and all of Malaysia. Although credit cards are routinely accepted at hotels, restaurants, and other bigger venues, it is advised to keep some local currency on hand for cash purchases.

Is a visa required to enter Penang?
A: Depending on your country of citizenship, you may need a visa to visit Penang. For a limited time, several nations are eligible for visa-free travel or visas that may be obtained upon arrival. It is essential

to confirm the precise visa requirements with the Malaysian embassy or consulate in your nation.

What modes of transportation are available in Penang?

A: There are several ways to get to Penang, including buses, taxis, ride-hailing services like Grab, rental automobiles, and motorbikes. You may also walk about Georgetown or take a trishaw for a more interesting means of transportation.

What are the top sights to see in Penang?

A: Penang is renowned for its historical and cultural landmarks, including Penang Hill, Kek Lok Si Temple, and the Georgetown Heritage Area. Other well-liked locations include Batu Ferringhi Beach, Penang National Park, and the city's famous street art murals.

What kind of food is served locally in Penang?

A: Penang is renowned for its tasty and varied food. Char Kway Teow, Penang Laksa, Nasi Kandar, and Hokkien Mee are a few foods you must taste. The island is renowned for its street food, with hawker centers providing a broad selection of inexpensive and delectable regional specialties.

Do you have any worries about safety in Penang?

A: Travelers may feel secure while visiting Penang. But it's always a good idea to follow standard safety procedures, including being alert to your surroundings, avoiding lonely locations at night, and keeping your possessions safe. Using licensed taxis or ride-hailing services is also advised for transportation.

What are some of Penang's well-liked retail districts?

A: The Batu Ferringhi Night Market, Gurney Plaza, Prangin Mall, and Straits Quay Marina Mall are a few of Penang's well-known shopping destinations. These locations provide a variety of shopping possibilities, ranging from local crafts and trinkets to well-known multinational brands.

Can I locate natives in Penang who speak English?

A: Yes, English is commonly spoken throughout Penang, particularly in hotels, restaurants, and retail establishments. It shouldn't be difficult for you to ask for help when you need it and communicate with the locals.

Please be aware that the details in this FAQ section are subject to change, so it is always a good idea to verify the most recent information and talk to official sources before visiting Penang.

Made in United States
Troutdale, OR
11/06/2023